SUCCESSFUL STRATEGIC PLANNING

Stephen G. Haines

A FIFTY-MINUTE™ SERIES BOOK

CRISP PUBLICATIONS, INC.
Menlo Park, California

SUCCESSFUL STRATEGIC PLANNING

Stephen G. Haines

CREDITS
Managing Editor: **Kathleen Barcos**
Editor: **Robert Racine**
Typesetting: **ExecuStaff**
Cover Design: **Carol Harris**
Artwork: **Ralph Mapson**

Copyright © 1995 by Crisp Publications, Inc.

Printed in the United States of America by Bawden Printing Company.

Distribution to the U.S. Trade:

National Book Network, Inc.
4720 Boston Way
Lanham, MD 20706
1-800-462-6420

Library of Congress Catalog Card Number 93-73141
Haines, Stephen G.
Successful Strategic Planning
ISBN 1-56052-251-8

This book is printed
on recyclable paper
with soy ink.

ABOUT THIS BOOK

Successful Strategic Planning presents a reinvented model of strategic planning for the twenty-first century. Its objective is to help teams, departments, and businesses of all sizes and types plan and implement strategies in an efficient, holistic, and integrated manner—in short, to become high-performance organizations. You will learn how to:

- Get educated and organized about strategic planning

- Develop a plan that identifies your ideal vision of the future, specific measures of success, and core strategies

- Ensure successful implementation

This "self-paced" workbook has numerous "action" assignments that teach you to write and reflect on all the key elements of a comprehensive strategic business plan.

ABOUT THE AUTHOR

Stephen G. Haines is an internationally recognized leader in the emerging field of Strategic Management and is the owner and founder of the Centre for Strategic Management. As a business strategist and facilitator of difficult executive groups, his background includes extensive board of director and senior executive experience in international and Fortune 500 firms, as a member of eight top management teams.

The highlight of his corporate career was Executive Vice President and Chief Administrative Officer of Imperial Corporation of America, a $13 billion nationwide financial services company.

He has also been president of University Associates Consulting and Training Services and is a 1968 graduate of the U.S. Naval Academy with multiple advanced degrees in Management, Human Resources and Organizational Development.

The Centre for Strategic Management
1420 Monitor Road
San Diego, CA 92110
(619) 275–6528 or Fax (619) 275–0324

Dedication

This book is dedicated to all my clients, from whom I have learned and continue to learn so much.

It is also dedicated to my wife, Jayne, the love of my life, whom I've known since high school. She is not only very understanding and supportive of my writings, but, as my business partner and business manager, has kept me superbly organized and happy in my work and my life.

Thank you all from the bottom of my heart!

CONTENTS

INTRODUCTION

Because strategic planning is a confusing and often discredited concept, we have researched and clarified what it is all about and demystified its terminology. A simple framework based on the following common-sense principles will show you how to strategically plan successfully and profitably.

First, planning is an integral part of management and leadership, not a fad, activity, or exercise to be completed and then abandoned. Planning should be part of a comprehensive strategic system guiding the day-to-day management of your lives and businesses toward achieving your vision.

Second, people support what they help create.
Thus, today's leadership and management practices, including strategic planning, must foster the involvement and participation at all levels that will create a critical mass for change. Otherwise, good plans will not get implemented. The only long-term competitive advantage that any organization can have today is its management style. Executives and managers must successfully lead in a proactive and participative way to unlock the ideas, skills, and motivation of their employees.

Third, true systems (or backward) thinking begins with defining your ideal vision of the future.
Then you think backward through the strategic steps that will accomplish that vision. This focus on desired outcomes distinguishes strategic planning from other forms of planning. Other forms merely move your business incrementally forward based only on your current direction and level of performance, not an ideal future vision.

Welcome to the world of strategic thinking and planning.

P A R T

I

Plan to Plan:
The Educating and
Organizing Step

*We must become architects of the
future, not defenders of the decline.*

GETTING STARTED WITH BACKWARDS THINKING

Every moment spent planning saves three to four in execution.

Strategic planning is often poorly accomplished, though not by intent or incompetence of planners, managers, and others. It is often due to a lack of preplanning; what we call Step 1: Plan to Plan. It is the educating and organizing step that is vital to engineering success up front before getting into the actual development of your strategic plan.

Strategic planning is a dynamic, backwards-thinking process by the collective leadership of the team, department or organization. They define their ideal future vision and core strategies necessary for consistent and meaningful annual operating plans and budgets. Then they drive the achievement and measurement of this vision.

Begin by conducting an Executive Briefing and Plan-to-Plan day. This allows everyone involved in your process to become educated and organized about strategic planning. This first step is often overlooked, with disastrous consequences later on when the planning process or its implementation fails.

Premise #1: Planning Is Part of Management

Any organization embarking on strategic planning must first decide if it is an event, a process, a change in roles, or a change in the way day-to-day business is run. While the complete answer is all of these, strategic planning must culminate in a significant change in the way daily business is conducted. This is an essential difference between our model and most others that end up not getting implemented.

To further understand how to proceed from good planning to successful day-to-day implementation of your plan, answer the following question:

Action: What are the five generally accepted functions of management (and where does planning fit in)?

1. _____
2. _____
3. _____
4. _____
5. _____

If you described planning, organizing, staffing, directing and controlling, in that order, you answered correctly.

GETTING STARTED WITH BACKWARDS THINKING (continued)

As simple as it might seem, most people have forgotten that planning is the primary function of management and should lead all of its other functions. The crush of other management fads and theories has caused us to lose sight of the basics. Remember, our goal is always to clarify and simplify.

Installing a management structure to implement strategic planning and change is the new way to run your business. Strategic plans are only blueprints; management's second step is to implement the plans and manage change based on a strategic plan, and system.

If you don't want anything to change, why bother to plan?

Our strategic planning and structure of managing change focuses on the difficult implementation of real change in the diverse behaviors that collectively make up an organization's culture. Making the customer the focus within an entire organization (or even within a team or department) requires continual reinforcement of new behaviors. You must counter the natural human tendency to repeat familiar behaviors and past habits. Thus, it cannot be stressed too early that strategic planning and managing change must be championed over the long haul by a single-minded dedication of the leaders doing the planning.

Although developing a strategic plan/document is an obvious first goal, the only true goal is ensuring its successful implementation.

Premise #2: People Support What They Help Create

Any team, department, or organization's first year of strategic planning involves setting in place the necessary plans and documents. A core planning team of 8 to 15 people from your collective leadership and key stakeholders (anyone with a stake in the success or failure of your plan) should lead the process, do the hard work, and make the decisions. A crucial task of the planning team is to hold consensus-building meetings involving the rest of management, staff, and other stakeholders.

Because people support what they help create, you should not plan in a vacuum. Instead, involve the people who matter to you (or who will help with implementation) as you plan. Gather their input as each draft document is developed as well as when it is finalized. If you wait until you are finished planning, others will be less likely to support you in implementation. In addition, you will get a host of new and different ideas to improve the quality of your plan.

The Parallel Process: Information-Sharing and Feedback Meetings

The best way to successfully involve others is through face-to-face discussions. Listing the following points up front will help you be focused and successful:

Parallel Process Meetings

Purposes:

- To explain the planning effort and your importance to it

- To explain our draft documents clearly to you

- To take your input back to the full planning team

Guarantee:

Your feedback will be seriously considered

Limitation:

Since input is being gathered from many people, it is impossible for each person's suggestions to be automatically placed into the final document.

The ability to generate active involvement of all key stakeholders via this parallel process requires professional skills practices by the collective leadership.

GETTING STARTED WITH BACKWARDS THINKING (continued)

Leadership Practices

Skills in being a good trainer, coach, and facilitator are now required to plan and implement strategically. Involvement, participation, and empowerment are the bywords. Leadership is all about specifying and inspiring a shared future vision, then enlisting and enabling others to act and be empowered in support of it.

Any planning process that does not include leaders being open to involvement and empowerment of others, as well as open to personal influence, will have serious problems with implementation. Without this give and take, the process of implementing your plan and managing change will encounter so much resistance (and continuation of the conceptual status quo) that the plan's success will be in jeopardy.

Each functional team of even the smallest organization *must* develop 12-month plans and budgets under this strategic plan umbrella. Developing these annual plans empowers leaders (and their teams) throughout the organization.

Finally, each individual in your team, department, or organization should be evaluated on

1. His or her contribution to the desired results (i.e., core strategies)

2. The behaviors (i.e., core values) specified and desired in your strategic plan.

The concept of linking levels of planning into a system is commonly overlooked; a serious omission. This linkage is what we call "strategic consistency, yet operational flexibility." It is the hallmark of good leadership and management practices.

Over the long term, good management and leadership is the only thing that distinguishes one organization from another.

Premise #3: Use Systems Thinking

Systems (or backward) thinking is a four-phase framework to "clarify and simplify" your planning and implementation. Earlier versions of strategic planning dealt mostly with the present and forecasted into the future. Today's planning, however, must begin with your future in mind. Why? It is a common-sense notion, just like knowing where you want to end up before you get into your car to drive somewhere.

Careful goal selection is the primary criterion of success in all the literature on organizations, teams, and individuals. This means first establishing a vision of your future as well as your purpose and meaning mission. Then finish your planning.

If we really want to create a high-performance organization, department, or team, planning and implementation must fit and work together as a system. The word "system" is, however, often overused and frequently misunderstood. To ensure that we are thinking alike, let's define it.

A system is made up of a set of components that work together for the overall objective of the whole (output).

Action: Diagram or draw in the space below the elements that describe any system (there are generally agreed to be five such elements).

GETTING STARTED WITH BACKWARDS THINKING (continued)

Now, compare your system with ours.

SYSTEMS THINKING

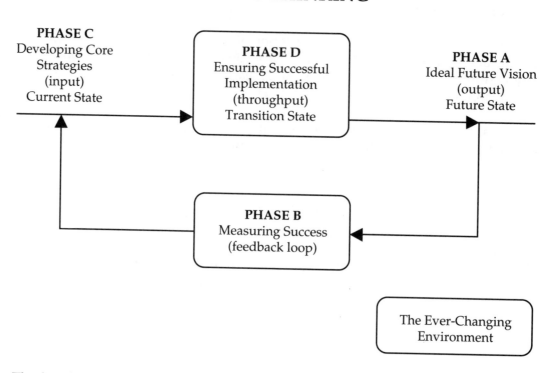

The first four of these elements correspond to the four phases of our strategic planning framework, the fifth being understood as the dynamic and ever-changing environment within which the system operates. We begin at Phase A, the ideal future vision we want to achieve (system output). Then, we work backward to the present and plan the strategies to achieve that vision.

Phase A: *Output* defines your ideal future success in your own terms: "Where do we want to be in the future at time X?"

Phase B: *Feedback loop* measures key factors and reports on the status of the results.

Phase C: *Inputs* of assessments of where you are today are the primary means to develop core strategies to achieve your ideal vision.

Phase D: *Throughput* consists of a set of specific actions to ensure successful implementation of your plan.

Strategic planning must start with the output (outcomes, ends, desired results or goals), since we want to be proactive in creating our ideal future. This is what distinguishes it from traditional long-range and other forms of planning. They usually start with the present—focusing primarily on problem-solving existing issues—rather than having a vision of success and profitability to achieve. They are piecemeal analytic approaches to a systems problem; they also fail to address the plan-to-implement step.

Phases A, B, C, and D and their sequence are true systems thinking and are essential to a high level of success. The following diagram illustrates these four phases and the ten steps (explained in detail in upcoming sections) of successful strategic planning.

The strategic planning model below is based on over five years of solid experience using it in the real world with many individuals, teams, departments and organizations.

Remember, an outcome-oriented system focuses on serving the customer.

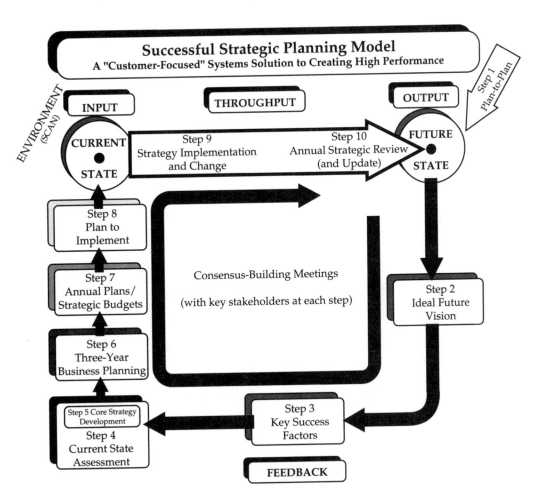

TODAY'S BUSINESS CLIMATE

The only limits, as always, are those of vision.

—Eleanor Roosevelt

We are in an era of revolutionary change. It is fundamental, radical, and global. These are incredible times of transformation typified by high growth and market opportunity; worldwide expansion and competition; corporate mergers, acquisitions, and other restructurings; and downsizing, obsolescence, and unforeseen events representing a shift in the business paradigm.

What are the implications of all this revolutionary change?

Action: Scan the environment around your own strategic planning entity. Consider social, competitive, economic, political, technical, industry, and customer influences.

Strategic Issues List

Answer the following questions individually and then discuss as a group.

What are the 3–6 environmental trends—projections—opportunities—threats facing us over the life of our strategic plan?	What are the 3–6 most important strategic issues facing us today as an organization?
1. _____	1. _____
2. _____	2. _____
3. _____	3. _____
4. _____	4. _____
5. _____	5. _____
6. _____	6. _____

To deal with these radical changes in our lives and careers, we must honestly join this transformation, since there is no resisting it. It is a time for new visions, strategies, programs, and actions—revolution, not evolution.

Goals

- Achieve success in this coming century; not just try and hold onto and prevent failure in our lives and careers

- Plan proactively for and take charge of our lives

- Create teamwork, much greater self-initiative, and empowerment under a clear vision

We need this clear direction and its corresponding accountability for faster, smarter, and innovative actions.

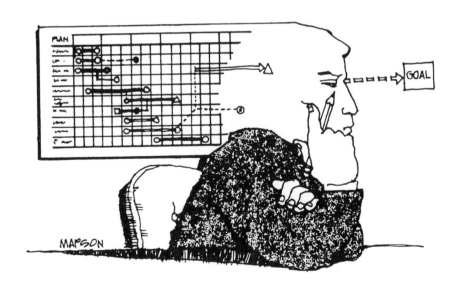

BENEFITS OF SYSTEMS THINKING AND STRATEGIC PLANNING

Our strategic planning model provides the following benefits:

1. A beginning visionary process encourages leaders to develop a shared vision of the future and to communicate core values and strategies. It aligns everyone's personal and professional goals to the same end—the customer. This empowers employees, reduces conflict, and makes decision making easier.

2. A set of specific and quantifiable measures can be developed that identify success (including customer satisfaction) year after year.

3. Stakeholders help to create your future, rather than being overwhelmed by and resistant to change.

4. You can proactively adapt to a changing global world and a turbulent marketplace. People and organizations can improve their competitive advantage over the competition by a thorough analysis of key success factors, environmental influences, and core strategies.

5. The planning team will learn to function as a highly effective executive team in support of the strategic plan. This modeling of cross-functional teamwork is essential to successful implementation of teams, departments, and organizations of any size.

6. This is an intensive development and strategic-orientation process for a new or aspiring executive, union leader, or team leader.

7. Setting priorities and focusing will help you determine precise budget cuts and spending priorities during tough employment, career, business, and economic times.

8. Executives, employees, and individuals alike will make sense out of today's confusing business strategies.

9. This is also a new way of thinking at the macro-strategic level, rather than the micro-operational level alone.

Action: List the top five benefits you will gain from strategic planning:

1. _____

2. _____

3. _____

4. _____

5. _____

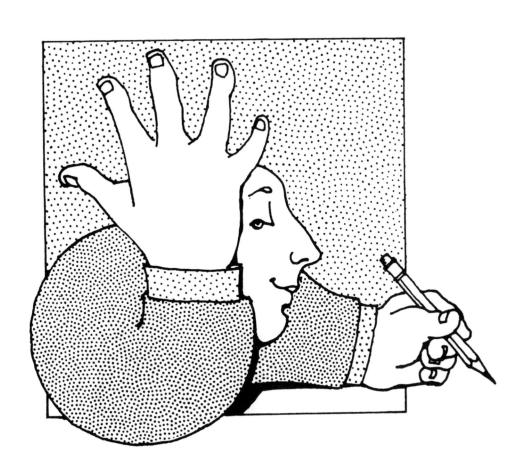

COMMON MISTAKES

Mistakes abound in strategic planning, such as:

► Failing to define your ideal future vision in the beginning

► Failing to clarify and simplify—Keep It Simple Simon (KISS)

► Failing to integrate planning at all levels

► Keeping planning separate from day-to-day management

► Developing only superficial vision, mission, and values statements

► Having yearly weekend retreats only and calling them strategic planning

► Failing to design/complete an effective implementation process

► Forgetting that people support what they help create

► Conducting "business as usual" after strategically planning otherwise

► Failing to make tough choices on future directions and obsolete tasks

► Lacking a scoreboard that measures what's important, not what's easy

► Having a scattershot and analytically oriented approach to planning as an activity

► Neglecting to gauge yourself against the competition

► Conducting only long-range financial forecasting

► Using confusing terminology and language

Action: Based on this list, what planning mistakes have you made in the past that you might make in the future unless you follow this system's approach?

1. _____

2. _____

3. _____

4. _____

OTHER CHOICES

Having seen the environmental changes going on all around you and having listed the strategic issues you face, what choice do you really have? The real question is not if, but how, you are going to address these issues.

Are you skeptical of the value of planning? If you are honest, you will probably be somewhat skeptical. Productive skepticism tells you the truth about what will work or not work in planning and implementation. So, listen to the skepticism and problem-solve the issues brought up. Those issues and barriers are your keys to successful implementation.

At this choice point, list your top 3–5 concerns.

Concerns/Barriers	Actions to Solve Concerns
1. _____	1. _____
2. _____	2. _____
3. _____	3. _____
4. _____	4. _____
5. _____	5. _____

STEP 1: PLAN TO PLAN

As you do Step 1: Plan to Plan, skepticism will keep you honest and ensure that any planning you do has a practical value and payoff. Hopefully, at this point, our system has laid to rest many of your unproductive reasons to be skeptical.

Action: What are you strategically planning for?

☐ **A.** A small- to medium-sized organization

☐ **B.** A department, team, or function

☐ **C.** A major project

Action: How long into the future are you planning for (3 years, 5 years, etc.)?

OTHER CHOICES (continued)

Action: Identify the key stakeholders you may want on your core planning team, those who will gain or lose by the success or failure of your strategic plan.

1. _____   9. _____

2. _____   10. _____

3. _____   11. _____

4. _____   12. _____

5. _____   13. _____

6. _____   14. _____

7. _____   15. _____

8. _____

Action: Circle the top 3–7 people that you must involve heavily in planning, the ones you will need a positive commitment from for successful implementation later.

Your planning team should include "all" members of your top management team. Invite a representative cross-section of key stakeholders to create a good give-and-take dialogue. However, strategic planning is not about being nice to each other, but having the right people in the room, working on the right (difficult) issues.

For effective group dynamics, 6–8 people are best, and 15 is the maximum to be productive. Groups larger than 15 people will probably require a professional facilitator.

Consider these personal qualities when choosing your planning team members:

- a clear sense of direction
- ownership and commitment (especially senior and middle management)
- key players with real information
- key informal leaders to help with successful implementation
- stakeholders with a broad perspective
- staff support group
- a mix of job and cultural diversity

Be sure they are willing to have an organization-wide perspective and orientation. The status quo, narrow perspectives and interests, and partisanship must be abandoned.

Strategic planning is not a collection of special interest groups, but individuals willing to collectively examine the team, department, or organization's ideal future in a holistic way. Defining and achieving your vision, mission, or purpose in today's changing environment is the paramount goal of your planning team.

Action: Now, list your core planning team members:

1. _____   8. _____

2. _____   9. _____

3. _____   10. _____

4. _____   11. _____

5. _____   12. _____

6. _____   13. _____

7. _____   14. _____

It may be helpful for each team member and your other stakeholders to have a copy of this book.

To work effectively, any group larger than 6–8 people probably needs a facilitator or trainer. Especially in planning, even with fewer than eight people, it is often more effective to have a facilitator guide the planning process, as well as handle the logistics/mechanics. Let members focus on the plan's content.

OTHER CHOICES (continued)

Action: It is important to be clear on how the planning team will make decisions. Determine if you are going to use the following consensus method or another decision-making method.

Consensus Decision Making

- Take the time we need.

- Do it as a team.

- Actively support the group decision, even if it not the exact one you would personally make.

- Present all sides to an issue in a full discussion, but limit time.

- Test for consensus.

- Focus on the substance of the discussion—the spirit or intent.

- Use prioritization techniques before discussions.

- Decision may be tentative (a draft) and subject to the validation/changes made by other key stakeholders, or a later, second review.

Based on your initial environmental scanning and strategic issues list (page 10), do you need to collect any further information or scan again?

Action: Document the environmental scanning already done on the following form.

Initial Environmental Scan

Instructions: List any additional initial environmental scanning that needs to be conducted at the beginning of the strategic planning process.

What areas were scanned/data collected?	Who was responsible?	When was it discussed?

IDENTIFY POTENTIAL BARRIERS TO THE STRATEGIC PLANNING PROCESS

Review the following list of potential barriers in the strategic planning process. Place a ✓ in boxes for items that you are encountering currently.

☐ Lack of senior management belief and commitment to planning or to the plan-to-plan step

☐ Group size too large or small to include the collective leadership

☐ No cultural belief in or rewards for planning

☐ No time/resource commitment to plan; unrealistic expectations; process rushed

☐ Day-to-day growth and pressures too dominant

☐ Adapting the strategic planning model to your unique situation

☐ Unwillingness to be visionary, proactive, and creative

☐ Avoidance of tough choices; failure to set priorities and focus budgets

☐ Reactive, low-risk, no rewards; low reinforcement for strategic thinking

☐ Difficulty in conceiving of factors to measure success

☐ Past history and mistakes in previous planning attempts

☐ Perseverance needed in completing the planning process itself

☐ Frequently changing priorities and focus; not persevering on one track; inconsistent decisions

☐ No management of implementation and process of change

☐ Difficulty in keeping up momentum in implementation

☐ Low commitment to the final products of the strategic plan

☐ Failure to provide the needed resources (financial and personnel) to implement

☐ Poor information on social, competitive, economic, political, technical, industry, and customer influences

☐ Differing directions/priorities among business/organizational units

☐ Conflicts, politics, lack of interpersonal skills among top management when working together

Readiness Steps and Actions

Complete the following list of steps and actions to ensure you have taken into consideration all the potential barriers to success.

What are the 3–5 most important readiness issues for us as an organization?	What prework or other actions should we take to cope with them?

You are now ready to design, build, and sustain a customer-focused, high-performance team, department and business.

II

Developing a Strategic Plan/Document

If you always do what you've always done, you'll always get what you've always gotten.

PHASE A: CREATING YOUR IDEAL FUTURE

Use backward thinking to begin creating your ideal future.

STEP 2: YOUR IDEAL FUTURE VISION

This is the place to actually begin strategic planning. By beginning at the end or desired outcomes and working backward, this step is concerned with formulating dreams that are worth believing in and fighting for. The cry "It can't be done!" is irrelevant.

The three challenges met in this step are to:

✓ **Develop a Vision Statement:**
 your shared hopes, dreams and shared image of the future.

✓ **Draft a Mission Statement:**
 why your organization exists, what business it's in, and whom it serves.

✓ **Articulate Core Values:**
 these will guide your day-to-day behavior and collectively create your desired organizational culture.

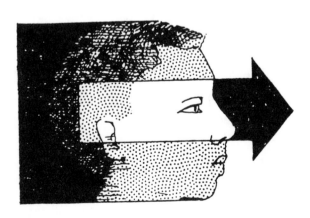

DEVELOP A VISION STATEMENT

If you are part of a larger organization, does it have its own future vision? If so, you may want to adopt it as your own and skip this vision exercise.

Action: Get yourself into a relaxed state and focus on the ideal future you want.

First, list your current boundaries using the following categories. They will help you identify the limits of your current thinking. Envision what your ideal future would be like without these limiting boundaries. Focus on your key desires and concepts, not on the exact wording just yet. Perfectionism and boundaries limit your ability to create your ideal.

Be Creative—Be Innovative—Be Limitless

Some Vision Boundaries

Possible Boundaries	Our Current Boundaries
• Specifics at a future year, decade, etc.	
• Our markets, customers	
• Our values, culture	
• Our core competencies and capabilities	
• Our driving forces, distinctive characteristics	
• Our geographic arena	
• Our history, environment, competitors, industry	
• Our governance (public, private, shareholders, not-for-profit, etc.)	
• Is it the ideal we want?	
• Answers the "why" we exist; do what we do; societal needs (i.e., goods/service to others)	
• Our level of leadership, excellence, service, quality, etc.	
• What we are known for; our reputation, image	

List your ideas of the ideal future vision at year _____ .

_____

_____

_____

_____

_____

_____

Once you have brainstormed your ideal future vision, then share it either with a 4–5 person subgroup or directly with the entire planning team. The goal of this challenge is to develop a consensus around one vision statement. Often it is important to first list a set of bullet statements for each concept that you can agree upon. From these, write a short, positive, and inspiring vision statement.

Our Vision Concepts

-
-
-
-
-
-
-
-

DEVELOP A VISION STATEMENT (continued)

From these bullet items, write a short, positive, and inspiring vision statement.

First Draft

_____

_____

_____

_____

_____

Second Draft (consensus)

_____

_____

_____

_____

_____

Now share this with your key stakeholders and gain their feedback to refine and finalize the document.

DRAFT A MISSION STATEMENT

A mission statement tends to be more realistic than a vision statement and answers three key questions: who, what and why. A fourth question, How do we operate?, is listed here to highlight what a mission is not. See the following Mission Development Triangle.

MISSION DEVELOPMENT TRIANGLE*

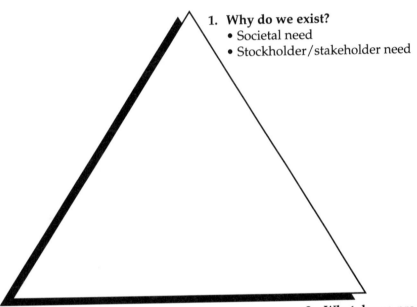

1. **Why do we exist?**
   - Societal need
   - Stockholder/stakeholder need

2. **Whom do we serve?**
   - Customers
   - Areas

3. **What do we produce?**
   - Products
   - Services

4. **How do we operate?**
   - Values, beliefs, philosophies
   - Major activities, techniques, support services
   - Technologies, methods of sale/distribution, capacity
   - Core competencies and capabilities

---

*Adapted from: P. Below, G. Morrisey, and B. Acomb, *Executive Guide to Strategic Planning*, 1978; S. Haines, *Internal Sun Co., Inc. Working Paper*, 1979; J. W. Pfeiffer, L. D. Goodstein, and T. M. Nolan, *Applied Strategic Planning: A How to Do It Guide*, Pfeiffer & Co., San Diego, CA, 1986.

Mission Development Exercise

Complete the exercise below individually. Don't worry about getting the perfect words yet. Just get your key concepts down on paper. Note that question 1, Why do we exist?, links back to your vision statement. Answer the questions for the way you want to be in the future in year _____ (end of the planning horizon).

1. Why do we exist (option: include this in your vision)?

_____

_____

_____

_____

2. Whom do we serve?

_____

_____

_____

3. What do we produce as outcome benefits?

_____

_____

_____

The fourth question, How do we operate?, cannot be answered until after you do work on your core values and strategies.

Action: Next, meet in subgroups or as a total planning team, and/or with key stakeholders and agree on your answers to the three questions.

Action: Now write your group mission statement: It should be

- feasible, understandable, and concise

- broad and continuing in nature, but not so broad as to be meaningless

- stated in terms of output (results) rather than activities (inputs or throughputs)

- worded specifically and purposefully (especially the names of your customers, products, and services)

Use these criteria while keeping the questions from the mission development triangle in mind.

For example: Our Mission is to serve . . . (customers) with the . . . (products and services) in order to achieve . . . (why we exist).

Our Mission is:

_____

_____

_____

_____

_____

_____

_____

_____

Now share this with your key stakeholders for feedback to refine and finalize the document.

DRAFT A MISSION STATEMENT (continued)

A clear customer definition is necessary since every team, department, and organization should have the purpose of serving someone else. Otherwise, the world would be in even more chaos than it is now, as everyone selfishly pursued his or her own needs. Our only true purpose is customer satisfaction.

"What goes around, comes around."

The fundamental truth of this statement often gets lost in the press of business and the stress of our personal lives. We cannot lose our service and customer focus.

Another key concept often gets lost in teams, departments, and organizations. We lose sight of the fact that our job is to serve the customer, *or* to serve someone else who does. Support teams and human resources (HR), finance, and legal departments sometimes resent their perceived secondary roles.

The point is not that others in the organization are any better than the support teams, but that others in the organization are their customers. The support team or department's job is to serve other employees, by which they serve the customer who buys your products and services.

Identifying, legitimizing, and resolving this dilemma is a key component of mission development. This is why consulting with other key stakeholders (including your internal and external customers) is so important.

To fully appreciate the concept of customer focus, we have developed the "Ten Commandments of Customer-Focused Organizations." Do you give lip service to this core concept or do you take it seriously?

Action: Reach a group consensus on your current state of being customer focused on a 1–10 scale (1 as low). Be honest; this exercise will tell you where you stand today, and what kind of future challenge awaits you in this area.

Ten Commandments of Customer-Focused Organizations

Rating Scale

_____ 1. Be close to the customer—especially senior executives (i.e., see, touch, feel, meet, and talk with them face to face on a regular basis). Include the customer in decisions, focus groups, meetings, planning, and deliberations.

_____ 2. Know the customers' needs, wants, and desires— continually, as they change—and surpass them with driving force.

_____ 3. Survey the customers' satisfaction with your products and services on a regular basis.

_____ 4. Focus on the "valued-added" benefits to the customer (quality and service, environmental respect, cost, and delivery response and speed, as well as performance, safety, and the intangibles).

_____ 5. Base your organization on customer input and focus; set quality standards for customer service—expectations that are specific and measurable in each department.

_____ 6. Require everyone in the organization to experience meeting and serving the customer directly, at least one day every year.

_____ 7. Focus and reengineer the business processes based on customer needs and perceptions—and do it across all functions.

_____ 8. Structure your organization by customer markets—1 customer = 1 representative.

_____ 9. Reward customer-focused behaviors (especially cross-functional teams that work together to serve the customer) and the heavy use of strategies to surpass customer expectations.

_____ 10. Hire and promote customer-friendly people.

ARTICULATE CORE VALUES

Core values guide our day-to-day behaviors and collectively create the desired culture of the organization. Sometimes called our beliefs and philosophies, they are few in number and usually meet the following criteria:

▶ They form a collective organization-wide belief. While individual values can be different, an organization requires values shared as a unit.

▶ They determine the norms or standards of acceptable behavior concerning how to approach your work.

▶ They are enduring and consistent over time. They are one of the last things you would want to give up (even in difficult times).

▶ They are driven by, and crystallized from, the top leadership in the entity.

*Organizational Values Exercise**

Complete Column 2: Select 10 of the following values that have the most importance to your organization's future success. Then complete Column 1 in the same way. Do this exercise individually.

	Column 1 The way it is now	Column 2 The way you think it should be
1. Long-term strategic perspective	☐	☐
2. Energizing leadership	☐	☐
3. Innovation/risk taking	☐	☐
4. Teamwork/collaboration	☐	☐
5. Recognition of achievements	☐	☐
6. Wise use of resources	☐	☐
7. Quality work/products/services	☐	☐
8. Contribution to society	☐	☐
9. Continuous improvement	☐	☐

	Column 1 The way it is now	Column 2 The way you think it should be
10. Safe and orderly environment	☐	☐
11. Positive organizational management	☐	☐
12. High staff productivity/performance	☐	☐
13. Customer service/sensitivity	☐	☐
14. Ethical and legal behavior	☐	☐
15. Stability/security	☐	☐
16. Profitability/cost consciousness	☐	☐
17. Employee development/growth	☐	☐
18. Organization growth	☐	☐
19. Openness/trust/positive confrontation	☐	☐
20. Respect/caring for individuals	☐	☐
21. Quality of work life	☐	☐
22. High staff satisfaction/morale	☐	☐
23. Decision making at lowest level	☐	☐
24. Employees involved prior to decisions	☐	☐
25. Employee self-initiative/freedom	☐	☐
26. Diversity and equal opportunity	☐	☐

*Adapted from S. Haines, *Internal Sun Co., Inc. Working Paper*, 1979; J. W. Pfeiffer, *Applied Strategic Planning: A How to Do It Guide*, 1986; and T. Rusk, *Ethical Persuasion Work Paper*, 1989.

ARTICULATE CORE VALUES (continued)

Action: Compare your answers with a subgroup or the full planning team. The goal is to develop a consensus for your desired organizational values (and a document to reflect that). You should agree on a small number (3–6) of these core values. Then, list the elements that fully define them in a useful way.

Action: Draft a list of your agreed-upon core values. On a separate piece of paper, list the key elements of each one.

Core Value: _____

Core Value: _____

Core Value: _____

Core Value: _____

Core Value: _____

Core Value: _____

You may want to assess how you are currently reinforcing these core values. See the following list of how core values *should* be used.

How Core Values Are Used

The following are typical ideas of how core values should appear and be reinforced within an organization. Examine this list and place a ✓ in the boxes by the 3–6 uses that you need to begin doing or to improve upon as a team, department or organization.

☐ Orientation and assimilation

☐ Job aids/descriptions

☐ Internal communication (vehicles/publications)

☐ Press releases, external publications, brochures

☐ Image nation-wide

☐ Recruiting handbook, selection criteria

☐ How applicants are treated (vs. values)

☐ How rewards for performance operate (vs. values), especially nonfinancial rewards

☐ Explicit corporate philosophy/values statement—visuals on walls

☐ Role of training/training programs (vs. values)

☐ Corporate and product advertising

☐ New customers and suppliers compared with current customer and supplier treatment and focus (vs. values)

☐ Performance evaluation/appraisal forms (assess values adherence)/team rewards

☐ New executive start-up

☐ Policies and procedures (HR, finance, administrative, etc.)/day-to-day decisions

☐ Cross-departmental events, flows, task forces

☐ To whom and how promotions occur (values consequence assessed)/criteria

☐ Executive leadership; ethical decisions, how we manage

☐ Dealing with difficult times/issues (i.e., layoffs, reorganizations)

☐ Strategy decisions

☐ Managing change

☐ Organization and job design

☐ Resource allocation

☐ Operational tasks of quality and service

☐ Stakeholder relationships

Where else should they appear and be reinforced within your organization?

1. _____

2. _____

3. _____

4. _____

5. _____

ARTICULATE CORE VALUES (continued)

Action: Share and compare your answers with others and develop a list of action items you need to do right away (*so you become an example immediately*).

Employees are usually not very tolerant of teams, departments, and organizations that don't fully follow their own values immediately, especially once those values are formally approved and rolled out to the organization. This important difference causes impatience regarding values. Employee response to this list of values may contrast with that of other strategic planning documents, which people realistically know and allow the time necessary for achievement.

No one can unrealistically expect the behavior of leaders to change overnight to match the new values; 12–18 months is often necessary to change behavior fully.

Action List—How to Improve Core Values

Core Value	What To Do?	By When?	By Whom?
•			
•			
•			
•			
•			

Now, share the Action List and the results of other Core Values actions with your key stakeholders for their feedback.

YOU ARE NOW READY TO IMPLEMENT PHASE B . . . READ ON!

PHASE B: MEASURING SUCCESS: TEN OR FEWER OUTCOMES

Goal setting and careful goal selection are the number one criteria for success in all the literature.

STEP 3 : KEY SUCCESS FACTORS

These are quantifiable outcome measures of success in achieving any team, department, or organization's vision, mission, and core values on a year-by-year basis.

This step is necessary to ensure that you are continually moving toward achieving your ideal future vision. Having concrete success factors will help you answer these critical questions during implementation:

► How do I know if I am being successful?

► How do I know if I am getting into trouble?

► If off course, what corrective actions should I take?

In developing your key success factors, first decide which areas define success for you.

If you want to do this step quickly, just use these four essential factors:

✓ **Customer Satisfaction**   ✓ **Employee Satisfaction**

✓ **Financial Results**   ✓ **Competitor Analysis**

What are the key phrases from your vision, mission, and core values that define success for you? Don't forget other key financial/operational areas.

_____

_____

_____

_____

PHASE B: MEASURING SUCCESS: TEN OR FEWER OUTCOMES (continued)

Once these areas are defined, specific measurements and yearly targets should be set. By limiting the number of measures to ten, you will focus on what's really important to your notion of success. A lack of focus is the major problem in almost all types of strategic planning. Key success factors should always measure what's really important (not just what's easy to measure). Typical customer satisfaction areas might include product quality, service, cost and value, speed, delivery and response time, as well as being environmentally responsive.

> *In the absence of clearly defined targets, we are forced to concentrate on activities and efforts . . . and we ultimately become enslaved by them.*

It is crucial to this step that you understand the different and innovative ways you can measure almost anything. Thus, success factors must be specific and quantifiable measures in one of four ways:

- quality (as perceived by the customer or internally with zero defects)

- quantity (production numbers or rates; the presence or absence of a program, product, etc.)

- time (quarterly or annually)

- cost

These quantifiable measures will show whether you have achieved success.

Action: For each area that defines success, set a measurable outcome target or success measure for the final year in your planning horizon. This should be a realistic target that you are deeply committed to achieving.

Focus on the vital few key outputs, not the many trivial activities. The operative concept is *key*, not comprehensive, success factors.

If your planning year is not far enough out into the future to actually achieve your ideal vision, consider using a column to distinguish your ultimate target as well. It helps keep your eye on your ideal. You may also find you have too many key success factors to be measured or just a comprehensive list of activities you are measuring. If so, go back and prioritize. Eliminate overlapping factors or those that are only the means to another outcome factor.

Key Success Factor	Baseline Year Target	Planning Horizon Year Target
1. _____		
2. _____		
3. _____		
4. _____		
5. _____		
6. _____		
7. _____		
8. _____		

Action: Once you have developed these factors and targets for your final planning year, it is time to develop your baseline target data for the current year.

Data is often missing, or does not exist for other than financial measures. This is normal. It is because you are being asked to measure what is important to your success, not what's easy to count. In some cases, success in the first baseline year consists of just two tasks: setting in place the measurement system and determining the success targets for the final year.

Action: Finally, set in place a system for measuring, tracking, and reporting these key success factors on a regular basis. This is the same as we do with monthly and quarterly budgets and financial statements. The only difference is that we are comparing the planned targets versus the actual results of all the key factors for success in our future vision, not just finances alone.

> *Financial measures and viability are necessary,*
> *but not sufficient, for success.*

Key success factors are pretty easy to describe and discuss. However, they are extremely difficult to develop qualitatively. Be sure to fine-tune your measures while you keep planning.

PHASE C: DEVELOPING AND CONVERTING STRATEGIES TO ACTIONS

"Organizations are successful, not because of the hundred and one good little actions they take to save money on paper clips and telephone calls, but because of one or two major strategies that are brilliant."

—Dr. Michael J. Kami

Phase C of our strategic planning model takes stock of current conditions and the status of your functioning today. Core strategies are then established to close the gap between the vision and today, along with a set of priority actions for the next year. These core strategies become the organizing framework to guide the rest of the planning process—from the strategic plan to the annual operational plan to the individual level of action and accountability.

STEP 4: CURRENT STATE ASSESSMENT

This is the first step of Phase C. The operative concept here is honesty.

While there are many ways to conduct an organizational assessment, the most clear and simple way is to conduct an analysis of your internal strengths and weaknesses and your external opportunities and threats. Then, examine the gaps between this analysis and the organization's vision for strategic and action implications.

In traditional forms of strategic planning, this step is the first and main step leading to long-range planning, which merely projects the current state of an organization incrementally (or "analytically") into the future.

Action: On the next page conduct an analysis of your strengths, weaknesses, opportunities, and threats. Do only the left-hand column of each category at first (we will discuss the right-hand side later).

If you are doing this analysis for a department or part of a larger organization, keep in mind that "external" means external to your department. In your case, there are two externals, one inside and one outside of your area within the larger organization. You may, therefore, decide to have two external analyses completed.

Internal Analysis

Strengths ("Build")	Action
1.	1.
2.	2.
3.	3.
4.	4.
5.	5.
6.	6.
7.	7.
8.	8.
9.	9.
10.	10.
Weaknesses ("Eliminate/Cope")	**Action**
1.	1.
2.	2.
3.	3.
4.	4.
5.	5.
6.	6.
7.	7.
8.	8.
9.	9.
10.	10.

External Analysis

Opportunities ("Exploit")	Action
1.	1.
2.	2.
3.	3.
4.	4.
5.	5.
6.	6.
7.	7.
8.	8.
9.	9.
10.	10.

Threats ("Ease/Lower")	Action
1.	1.
2.	2.
3.	3.
4.	4.
5.	5.
6.	6.
7.	7.
8.	8.
9.	9.
10.	10.

Action: Once you have analyzed your current state, review it with a subgroup, the whole planning team, and finally with your key stakeholders. Make additions or corrections as necessary. You may find that some issues have both strengths and weaknesses.

Action: Now, go back to your analysis and fill in the Actions required by each item listed (the right-hand column).

You should be able to brainstorm at least one action for each item you listed in the left column. It is not necessary to agree on all these actions. They are just initial thoughts to develop core strategies and their actions and priorities.

STEP 5: CORE STRATEGY DEVELOPMENT

Core strategy development bridges the gap between your ideal future vision and your current state.

This step should focus on 3–7 core strategies to be implemented by the team, department, or organization. You need a focused set of strategies as the primary means to achieve your ideal future vision. These strategies become the organizing principles and priorities used by everyone as a framework to set annual organizational, department/team, and individual goals and actions.

The 1990s have seen a proliferation of new strategies as businesses try to cope with these revolutionary times. They include:

- Flexibility and opportunism in looking for bargains
- Business process reengineering
- High-speed product development
- Horizontal integration of related products and by-products
- Networks, partnerships, and alliances
- Value-added consumer bargains
- Environmentally based or improved products
- Mass customization

PHASE C: DEVELOPING AND CONVERTING STRATEGIES TO ACTIONS (continued)

These new strategies are in addition to the ones that have been popular in the 1980s, including: total quality management, empowerment, self-directed work teams, visionary leadership, customer service, capital leverage, divestitures, retrenchments, and cost reductions.

Beware of strategies that are only cost-cutting measures. These might include reorganizations, layoffs, business reengineering, and budget cutbacks. Cutting is definitely necessary, but not sufficient for success. Long-term strategies that build for the future focus on quality products and services that satisfy the customer. Cutting and building strategies are both needed.

Action: What are the 3–7 (maximum) core strategies you should pursue over the life of your planning horizon to achieve your ideal future vision?

Use the preceding lists and the analysis of your current state (including its required Actions) to help.

1. _____

2. _____

3. _____

4. _____

5. _____

6. _____

7. _____

Action: Refine this list of core strategies thoroughly with either a subgroup or the full planning team, and then with your other key stakeholders to ensure consensus.

Be sure to write these core strategies in the active tense, with an action verb and as a complete sentence. It must be crystal clear what actions you desire. If you did your planning process thoroughly up to this point, this list shouldn't be a problem to develop. You have probably been discussing them informally throughout the planning process as you developed earlier documents.

The fewer the number of core strategies, the better. Making tough choices here in order to focus is essential to success in almost all strategic planning. Teams, departments, and organizations that try to be "all things to all people" rarely succeed.

CHANGES IN YOUR CORE STRATEGIES

Since core strategies are crucial to success and profitability, it is not enough to have a good list of strategies in an active format and wording. In addition, a clear list of specific changes that these strategies entail is crucial.

Action: Complete the following list of changing core strategies (new or improved) and those that are continuing the same.

Changing Core Strategies

From

To

1. _____   1. _____

2. _____   2. _____

3. _____   3. _____

4. _____   4. _____

5. _____   5. _____

Continuing Core Strategies

1. _____

2. _____

3. _____

4. _____

5. _____

STRATEGIC ACTIONS

Action: On separate pieces of paper develop 5–15 actions (activities, organizational priorities, changes) to accomplish during the planning horizon to achieve each core strategy.

Action: From the previous list further identify (with an asterisk) the top 2–4 action priorities for each core strategy over the next fiscal year. These provide direction for everyone in setting their team, department, section, and individual goals for the coming year.

At this point you have completed the basic phases and steps in strategic planning and backward thinking in the narrow sense of traditional planning (but not in our definition, though). Now it is time to cascade the strategic plan down to annual plans and budgets and eventually to individual performance appraisals.

STEP 6: THREE-YEAR BUSINESS PLANNING

This step is not applicable in this book. The three-year business plan applies only to large corporations with multiple strategic business units where they need to develop three-year business plans under the context of the overall strategic plan. For more information, contact the author directly.

STEP 7: ANNUAL PLANS AND STRATEGIC BUDGETS

Annual plans and strategic budgets is where "the rubber meets the road."

Excellence is a matter of doing 10,000 things right.

Begin by developing department or section plans for the next fiscal year. You also prioritize your tasks for the year and then provide the resources to implement your core strategies.

Action: Each department or unit in the entity you are planning for should fill out an Annual Plan for each core strategy.

Consistency in organizing all departments, teams, and sections under the same core strategies is the key to an integrated and thorough implementation. This cannot be stressed enough. By doing so, you will begin to think about achieving strategies to serve your customers rather than thinking about unit objectives and turf battles. For small teams completing this strategic planning process, it may be enough for you to complete one set of annual plans for the entire team.

Unit Name: _____

Date: _____
Fiscal Year: _____

Annual Plan

Strategy #: _____

Strategic Action (actions/objectives/how?)	Support/resources needed	Who is responsible?	Who else to involve?	When done?	How to measure?	Status

(If you need more forms to work this annual planning, this page may be reproduced without further permission from the publisher.)

STRATEGIC ACTIONS (continued)

Large Group Review

Action: It is not enough to have each team, department, unit, or section develop their own annual plans in isolation from others on the planning team. You also need a large-group annual review meeting of the full collective leadership (10–50 people can attend—possibly the entire department). At this meeting, all annual unit plans are shared, critiqued, and refined, based on their integrity to the yearly top priorities for each core strategy.

Strategic Budgeting

Once you have completed your annual plans, then it is time to change the way budgeting is traditionally done. Good strategic budgeting needs to follow (not lead) annual planning. This will enable you to achieve a more focused allocation of resources based on the strategic plan.

This also produces a tension between current allocations and future action priorities, which is normal and desired. It helps you focus time and energy toward your top future priorities (defined at the end of Step 5) versus just spending your limited resources in past habitual ways. It is important that you build a budget that focuses on your top 2–4 priorities for each core strategy. Hence, the importance of the column "support/resources needed" on the annual plan.

Action: A sample "resource allocation plan" and format is provided for your information. For those of you who are seriously concerned about the funding of your core strategies and action priorities, this is a good model to follow.

Resource Allocation Plan

Instructions: Based on forecasted revenues/budget availability, conduct a "Resource Allocation Plan" using this pro forma matrix as a guide. Do not add/delete the same budget % for each department, but rather add/delete resources based on the core strategies.

What % of revenue/budget?

1. Marketing/sales expense _____ %

2. Costs of goods sold _____ %

3. General and administrative expenses _____ %

4. _____ %

5. _____ %

6. _____ %

7. _____ %

8. _____ %

9. RFP* funds set aside to further strategic planning pilot projects _____ %

10. Profit/retained earnings _____ %

TOTAL OF REVENUE/BUDGET 100%

_____

*RFP—"Request for Proposal" is an excellent way to reward employees who want to support and further the strategic direction of the organization. Even a small percent held in reserve is important.

STRATEGIC ACTIONS (continued)

The 1990s seem destined to be remembered for economic difficulties and the lack of funding and revenues to operate. This seems to be the case for both public and private organizations across North America.

While it is not the purpose of this book to take you fully through strategic budgeting, we present 10 approaches regarding resource allocation and tight budgets.

Ten Ways to Approach Resource Allocation

"If money was what it took to be a success, then how did Japan and Germany rise from the ashes?"

—Anonymous

Approach #1: Macro allocations

Consider macro allocation by top management for each strategic business unit/ major support department (i.e., a pie chart). Require reallocation within existing department resources to respond to new priorities (but be sure to allow more flexibility to switch funding and priorities).

Approach #2: Activity level budgeting

Reexamine your organizational priorities at the "activity level," focusing all the way through the organization. Have everyone force rank their activities/projects/ programs, along with budget and people cost implications.

Approach #3: Require 5–10–15% budget cut projections and plans

Ask for projected cuts of 5%, of 10%, and of 15% from each department, along with what plans/projects will be affected. Then cut departments *individually* and in *different amounts* based on your strategic priorities. Keep in mind that across-the-board cuts "take no management skills and are just a coward's way out of tough choices."

Approach #4: Budget "hold-backs"

Set aside X% (i.e., 2–5%) of your budget to create a pool of funds for strategic priorities within existing budgets, as well as to further new pilot programs/experiments to take you toward your vision of the future.

Approach #5: New initiative programs

Have your employees recommend new initiative programs/projects that tie directly to the criteria in your strategic plan. Make sure budget and people costs/rationale are associated with each one. You can use this for all new funding above last year's as well.

Note: The next five approaches should be started earlier in the year, so that their results in cost savings will be evident at budgeting time.

Approach #6: Work out the bureaucracy

Set up a broader reengineering process:

- Eliminate bureaucracy
- Empower and delegate to staff
- Streamline work flow inefficiencies
- Eliminate "waste" within your departments

Approach #7: Reengineer your business's economic structure/processes

Make major structural changes in the way you do business to lower cost (i.e., "aides" vs. full-fledged professionals). Doing more with less is what the 1990s are all about, but there are ways to approach this with foresight.

- Flatten your organization by continuously empowering employees.
- Lower manufacturing costs on non-value-added items.
- Radically reengineer your customer-focused business processes to be more streamlined, quicker, and lower in cost.
- Know your customer's priorities.
- Know and implement your span of control.
- Keep statistics—they'll flag patterns and give a historical perspective.

STRATEGIC ACTIONS (continued)

Approach #8: Learning as a critical resource (increase skills and motivation)

Invest some time and energy in your most critical resource—learning. Are there other ways the existing HR could be used to achieve your vision—such as focus, motivation, commitment, new knowledge, technology, innovation and creativity, best practices emulation, leverage, or continuous improvement projects? Most organizations still treat people as a fixed asset with a fixed cost, rather than as a variable-output human element.

Approach #9: Recognition and reward programs

Set up a "recognition program" rewarding actual documented cost savings, not suggestions. Suggestions are a dime a dozen—it's actual cost savings you really want.

Approach #10: Fund-raising

Start fund-raising as one of your important organizational functions. Acquire endowments/annuities for long-term funding. Recommend new ways to increase revenue, such as fund drives, alternative sources of funds, or "in-kind" donations and grants.

P A R T

III

Plan to Implement

Change takes 3–5 years, even with concentrated and continual actions.

PHASE D: IMPLEMENTING CHANGE SUCCESSFULLY

Proper planning prevents poor performance.

This phase does not concern strategic planning, but rather the beginning of successful implementation (Goal #2). However, in using the system's thinking model and process, it is clear that there are two goals to accomplish. Now it is time to focus exclusively on the second of these: ensuring successful implementation of your strategic plan. None of the various strategic planning models mentioned earlier have the following step.

STEP 8: PLAN TO IMPLEMENT

This step focuses on the process of educating and organizing to manage the implementation of the strategic plan. Thus, it deals with that difficult subject—change.

EDUCATIONAL BRIEFING ON CHANGE

The first thing to appreciate is how we experience change. The "Roller Coaster of Change" diagram simplifies and clarifies the basic psychology of individual and organizational change.

ROLLERCOASTER OF CHANGE

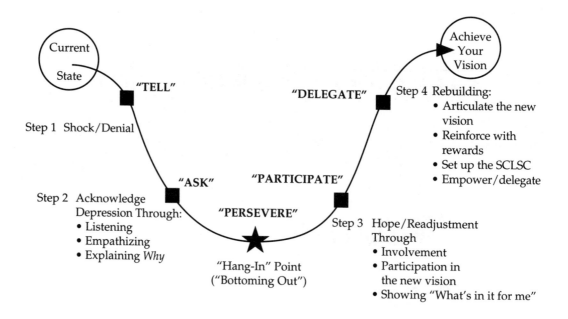

Action: Study this model's four basic steps, keeping in mind that the reality of change is much more complex. Each employee goes through this at his or her own pace and depth in a process that must be managed. We often undergo a number of different changes at the same time (personal, professional, social, and spiritual). Focus on the bottoming-out point, where success or failure is often decided. When times get tough, perseverance and discipline in your thinking and acting are needed.

Questions to Address

There are major questions that you should keep in mind when implementing your changes in the core strategies.

1. Not "if" but "when" will we start to go through shock/depression?

2. How deep is the trough? Is it different for each person? What are the implications?

3. How long does the trough take? Are employees and management at the same stage of change at the same time?

4. How do we manage change proactively?

5. Will we rebuild and fully achieve our vision?

6. At what level will we rebuild?

7. What new skills do we need to accomplish this?

8. How may different roller coasters will we experience in this change?

9. Are there other changes occurring at the same time for people?

10. Will we hang in and persevere at the bottom? How?

11. How will we deal with normal resistance?

12. How will we create a critical mass to support and achieve the desired changes?

Action: Discuss these questions of change fully among a subgroup, the full planning team, and your other key stakeholders.

EDUCATIONAL BRIEFING (continued)

Action: Make a list of the agreed-upon key points on change that will guide your implementation.

Key Points on Change

1. _____

2. _____

3. _____

4. _____

5. _____

ORGANIZING FOR IMPLEMENTATION

*What we think, know, or believe is, in the end, of little consequence.
The only consequence . . . is what we do.*

Action: Use the prototype below to review and finalize your strategic planning document for use in a practical day-to-day fashion.

Strategic Planning Document

Sections/Documents

I. Introduction   3–6 pages

1. Cover sheet
2. Executive summary history
3. Strategic planning model
4. Acknowledgments
5. Table of contents
6. Environmental scanning and strategic issues

II. Ideal Future Vision and Strategies   12–15 pages

1. Vision/back-up elements
2. Mission
3. Core values/back-up elements
4. Key success factors/first year action plan
5. Current-state assessment
6. Three-year business plan (if applicable)
7. Core strategies and top priority actions
8. Annual plans and strategic budgeting

III. Implementation   2–4 pages

1. Summary of the leadership steering committee
2. Year #1 task checklist and schedule of implementation

TOTAL   **17–25 pages**

Now decide how you will communicate your plan to all your key stakeholders.

ORGANIZING FOR IMPLEMENTATION (continued)

Ideas for Initially Communicating the Strategic Plan

▶ Print the plan and distribute it with a simple cover letter.

▶ Develop handouts/overhead slides for standardized use by all executives.

▶ Hold an organization-wide managers' meeting to hear directly from the CEO/executive director and other members of the planning team (thank them for their help).

▶ Organize divisional/departmental all-employee meetings to ask questions about the plan and to pose concerns.

▶ Set up stakeholder meetings to review results and thank them for their help.

▶ Hold 2-day workshops to learn about strategic planning, to discuss the plan, and to build supporting plans at a unit/site or individual level.

▶ Implement a mini strategic planning process for units.

▶ Display posters with planning themes.

▶ Hand out individual (plastic) cards with values, mission, and key success factors.

▶ Produce video tapes of the CEO/executive director (or others) explaining the organization's vision and strategies to achieve that vision.

▶ Publish an internal newsletter, memo, or letter to introduce the plan (overall and in detail).

▶ Publish external news releases and special public feature stories.

▶ Give out report cards each quarter—shared with all stakeholders.

> Now: How do we keep the plan alive over the next 3–5 years?

Action: Use this set of ideas as a guide to develop your communications game plan:

Communications to do	By Whom?	By When?
•		
•		
•		
•		
•		

To achieve your desired changes, each leader must also manage two common problems. First, changes must be nurtured, protected, encouraged, and rewarded in order to be achieved. Second, despite good intentions, the crises of day-to-day living and working drive out the focus on change, so that it is often never fully implemented.

Action: Set up a strategic change leadership steering committee to combat these problems by guiding the changes dictated by the plan and establishing a yearly map to manage the change and implementation processes over the life of the planning horizon.

THE LEADERSHIP STEERING COMMITTEE: KEY TO SUCCESS

Changing behavior always requires deep feelings.

The strategic change leadership steering committee is essential in successfully and profitably implementing your strategic plan. Implementation will fail without it. We have to manage change before it manages us.

Steering Committee Guidelines

A new way to run your business, giving equal weight to changes and to the ongoing daily management of the organization.

Purposes

1. To guide and control the implementation of any large-scale, organization-wide strategic planning/change undertaken.
2. To coordinate any other major performance improvement projects going on at the same time; to ensure fit with the time and energy demands of ongoing daily business activities.

Committee Meeting Frequency

1. Monthly or bimonthly as the process begins.
2. Quarterly once the process is functioning smoothly (but more frequently the faster you want to implement).

Criteria for Membership

1. Senior management leadership teams for today and the future.
2. Informal or formal leaders from parts of the organization that are essential to implementation.
3. Core steering group members including the coordinator managing change, the key success factor coordinator, and internal facilitators.
4. Credible staff who understand the strategic plan developed.
5. Key stakeholders who share your vision and are willing to actively support it.

In addition to the committee itself, you also need to define a core steering group to manage the implementation process on a weekly and day-to-day level. One of the things the group can do is compile a list of the top priority actions under each strategy for this current year and manage them closely.

In other words, it should become *"the new way to run your business and life day-to-day."*

Action: Define your strategic change leadership steering committee parameters below.

1. Committee purpose: _____

2. Committee membership:

   _____   _____

   _____   _____

   _____   _____

   _____   _____

   _____

3. Steering group core members: _____

   _____

   _____

4. Specific involvement of your middle and first line supervisors (and other

   key players): _____

   _____

   _____

   _____

5. Meeting frequency/length: _____

6. Meeting location offsite: _____

7. Communications to and involvement of other stakeholders: _____

   _____

   _____

THE LEADERSHIP STEERING COMMITTEE: KEY TO SUCCESS (continued)

The leadership steering committee and the planning team are very similar, their guidelines being almost alike:

- led by top management

- about 80–90% same membership

- size normally 15 or fewer members

- use of the consensus process and written communications after every meeting

The frequency and intensity of the steering committee meetings are less than those of the planning team. You should be putting all your energies into implementation tasks rather than meetings.

Steering committees typically hold one-day meetings in medium- to large-size departments, business units, and organizations. Such meetings must be held regularly in order to pull back from the day-to-day activities, scan the landscape and status of the strategic plan, and replan its implementation as necessary.

You should institute a steering group to manage the implementation process on a weekly and day-to-day level. The group can compile a list of the top-priority actions under each strategy for the current year and manage them closely.

Summarize the parameters of the steering committee and insert it at the back of your formal strategic planning document. Use the following minimum agenda of mandatory items as a template for your meetings:

▶ Continually scan the changing environment for plan implications.

▶ Track, report and problem-solve key issues concerning Key Success Factors.

▶ Report and problem-solve any issues concerning the core strategies and their top-priority actions.

Finally, the steering committee should establish a task checklist to ensure implementation of the plan, particularly until the first year's new changes are completed.

Action: As a group, complete the first year's task checklist and add to it a month-by-month schedule of implementation meetings and activities to occur during the first year.

Year #1: Task Checklist

☐ Finalize the strategic plan and develop an initial communications plan.

☐ Establish an organization-wide annual plan reflecting the action priorities for each core strategy.

☐ Align the budget to reflect the annual priorities (to be at least 33% effective in the first year—i.e., strategic budgeting).

☐ Build all department/division/unit annual plans around the organization-wide annual priorities/goals. Hold a peer review of them.

☐ (Optional) Implement three-year business plans for each strategic business unit/master support division/executive via mini strategic plans (over the next 12 months?) to verify, extend, and integrate the organization-wide plan.

☐ Set up an ongoing leadership steering committee to manage the change process (meet bimonthly at first, then quarterly).

☐ Establish a task checklist for implementation and follow-up (month-by-month schedule).

☐ Establish a system/coordinator to monitor, track, and report key success factors.

☐ Revise the performance management/appraisal and reward systems to support the desired vision.

☐ Examine your organizational structure as well as staff/succession planning to support the desired vision.

☐ Implement the desired change(s) in both the headquarters' departments and in units/sites/field locations.

☐ Put in place an environmental scanning system.

☐ Establish senior management's personal commitment to a set of tasks to lead implementation of the strategic plan.

THE LEADERSHIP STEERING COMMITTEE: KEY TO SUCCESS (continued)

☐ Set up internal staff to build your internal expert group with the skills (not just knowledge) to carry out your vision and core values.

☐ Ensure that key cross-departmental "Strategic Change Projects" are set up with clear accountability.

☐ Establish a critical mass for change (rational, political, cultural).

☐ Put teams in place to sponsor each core strategy.

☐ Direct resource allocation to fund the change process.

☐ Have two absolutely key training and development programs in place with a top-down fashion (a) Mastering Strategic Change, and (b) Visionary Leadership Practices and Skills.

☐ Set up the dates for the annual strategic review (and update).

Add this schedule to your strategic planning document.

Obviously, not all of these steps must be included in everyone's game plan. However, everyone should have a game plan to combat the failure to live up to their good intentions.

Teams, departments, business units, and organizations should be careful not to be "penny-wise and pound foolish." Don't fall prey to the tendency to put all your time, energies, and resources into planning and assume that the implementation will naturally follow. The failure to bridge the gap between planning and implementation can be a major problem. If your plan truly represents your top priorities, then use it, don't abandon it.

STEP 9: STRATEGY IMPLEMENTATION AND CHANGE

People do what we inspect . . . not what we expect.
—Stephen Haines

To be successful, a strategic plan must be transformed into hundreds of positive individual plans and efforts, with a rewards and recognition system. This level of team, department, and organization integrity in support of your vision is difficult to achieve. It takes leadership and focus. Your belief that you can do it will lead to actions, which is the bottom line of strategic planning.

The leadership steering committee must lead the implementation by following up and correcting mistakes, and by bringing disciplined persistence and integrity to the plan.

Some people may not like the preceding quote on inspect versus expect. It *is* quite harsh, but the failure to understand this is a sickness of management today, in all types of organizations. While high expectations are nice, many managers are afraid to inspect and hold people accountable for performance.

Note: When companies choose not to establish a steering committee to ensure follow-up and inspection, they usually later need assistance conducting the last step in planning: an annual strategic review. They find that they need to install a steering committee and restart their stalled implementation after all. Once these meetings are organized and held, implementation, follow-up, inspection, and results pick up speed.

THE LEADERSHIP STEERING COMMITTEE: KEY TO SUCCESS (continued)

STEP 10: ANNUAL STRATEGIC REVIEW (AND UPDATE)

This is similar to a yearly independent financial audit. It has two goals:

- Assess the status of how well your strategic plan has been achieved.

- Assess the implementation of your system of managing change.

This review has three main tasks:

- Reacting to changes in the environment and their implications for updating your core strategies.

- Update annual action priorities for the next 12 months for each core strategy and hold the annual large-group review meeting.

- Update your leadership steering committee's plan for success and its system for managing change.

At this point you should have developed an excellent strategic plan for your entity. Now, your main "planning task" is to review and update it annually only as necessary, not redo it.

The annual task is now one of verifying your vision, mission, and core values, as well as checking your key success factors and core strategies, while completely redoing your current state assessment yearly plans, priorities, and budgets. It is crucial to strategically manage the plan you have created.

ANNUAL REVIEW AND UPDATE

Instructions: Based on the framework below (#1 and #2), each organization needs to conduct a yearly follow-up and diagnosis on how they are performing. This is key to "learning to be a high-performance organization."

Strategic Management System (SMS)

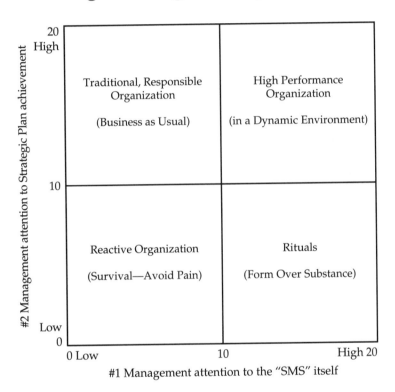

Summary

It is important for people to develop strategic plans for their teams, departments and businesses. However, once these plans are developed, it is crucial to have a system of managing strategically from these plans. Hence, the last piece of Successful Strategic Planning goes by the same name: Strategic Management System (SMS). All of your prework, planning, implementing, and updating steps are what we mean by the Two-Part Strategic Management System as the new way to run your business.

For a visual representation of this Strategic Management System and its Annual Strategic Review (and Update), see the diagram on the next page.

Two-Part Strategic Management Systems Solution

PART I: GOAL 1

Phases A, B, C: Develop a Strategic Plan/Document

STEP 1: Plan to Plan (Educate and Organize for Planning)

- ✓ Organizational Diagnosis
- ✓ Executive Briefing
- ✓ Plan to Plan Tasks
- ✓ Visionary Leadership
- ✓ Team Building

STEPS 2–7: Strategic Design

- ✓ Conduct Strategic Planning
- ✓ Competitive Strategies
- ✓ Customer Focused
- ✓ Annual Plans/Strategic Budgets

STEP 8: Plan to Implement (Educate and Organize for Change)

- ✓ Bridging the Gap

PART II: GOAL 2

Phase D: Ensure Successful Implementation

STEP 9: Build Changes

- ✓ Implementing Strategic Change
- ✓ Leadership Steering Committee

STEP 10: Sustain Performance

- ✓ Annual Strategic Review (and Update): Independent Evaluation
- ✓ Increased Team Building
- ✓ Increased Leadership Development

**Bottom Line: Create and Sustain a Customer-Focused
High-Performance Organization**

P A R T

IV

Facilitator Tips to Ensure Success

You can, and should, shape your own future because if you don't, somebody else surely will.

FACILITATOR TIPS

The following tips are for those planners, trainers, and consultants who want to teach or facilitate strategic planning efforts.

Tip #1 The first items on any meeting agenda are a clear purpose and time frame.

Tip #2 Be sure to get agreement and understanding from all planning team members each step of the way. Consensus decision making works best.

Tip #3 To reach a consensus, answer these questions:

- How and with whom are you going to communicate?

- What documents do you want to get feedback on?

- Whose job is it to communicate and when does it have to be completed by?

- In what usable form will feedback come to the next meeting?

- How will you deal with the normal skeptics as you seek consensus?

- Are you really willing to hear, listen, and act on the feedback you receive?

- What other consensus-forming elements do you need to identify and resolve?

Tip #4 The analysis of your current state (strengths, weaknesses, opportunities, threats) is an excellent way to first involve many key stakeholders in the process of reaching consensus. Decide whether others outside the planning team can develop this analysis (and action implications too).

Tip #5 If the analysis of your current state is done by key stakeholders, the planning team's task would be to review and refine the analysis and action implications presented.

FACILITATOR TIPS (continued)

Tip #6 Do each planning exercise individually first. Then, share and compare it with other planning team members to reach a consensus decision. If your planning group contains 10–15 people, in keeping with effective group dynamics you may use intermediate steps with 3 subgroups of about 4–5 people.

Tip #7 An alternative way to begin drafting your ideal future vision is to do the personal values exercise in building openness, trust, and team spirit.

Tip #8 In developing key success factors, appoint a coordinator to develop, track, and measure these factors and report them to the steering committee on a regular basis. Achieving high ratings on these factors is *not* this coordinator's role. It lies with the collective leadership and top management.

Tip #9 A standard for meetings is every 4–6 weeks, to allow time for reflection.

Tip #10 Make sure the leadership roles are clear and that the responsible person in your unit is fully in charge. Delegating planning to the facilitator or someone else is actually an abdication of the job and will *not* produce the ownership needed for successful implementation.

Tip #11 Encourage skepticism in the group so that you bring to light and problem-solve all resistance and barriers to success.

Tip #12 Don't react to posturing and polarizing statements. Ask for the reasoning behind people's opinions. The key role of the facilitator is to expand the range of information available to the planning team.

Tip #13 Each group has its own pace, which you can help clarify or modify.

Tip #14 The best documents are free of jargon and state direction and decisions in plain English, particularly your first drafts that will be circulated in building consensus.

Tip #15 Balancing between content and process; know when to confront and when to back off.

Tip #16 If things always go smoothly, you are not getting to the tough issues that require slugging-it-out perseverance.

Tip #17 The facilitator's grip on the process should be neither loose nor tight; ownership and decisions continue to stay with the collective leadership.

Tip #18 Building the planning document as you go is easier and gives a positive view of progress.

Tip #19 Make liberal use of flip charts to demonstrate, focus discussions, test conclusions, sum up decisions, and give instructions.

Tip #20 Be careful in adding new members to a planning team once you get started. You'll need to back up and slow down to help them join in.

Tip #21 Use three subgroups (not two) to minimize "we-they" discussions, and use volunteers for some subgroups to increase ownership of the results.

Tip #22 Facilitating planning group closure is a difficult task and should include active listening, summing up discussions accurately, testing for closure, and recording decisions in writing.

Tip #23 Priority-setting is the key to success in all strategic planning. Forced ranking (or at least limiting priorities to the top three in rank) constitutes prioritizing, not categorizing as high–medium–low.

NOTES

NOTES

NOTES

NOTES